IMAGES OF ENGLAND

Standish & Shevington

Chancel screen in St Wilfrid's parish church, Standish, soon after the addition of the heraldic shields by Rector Hutton in 1917. Designed by Austin & Paley, the whole series represents families from the eleven original townships of the parish. The six shown here are: Langtree, Standish of Standish (old and new), Standish of Duxbury, Burgh and Rigby. The three 'tuns' or dishes are instantly recognizable to locals as the Standish family's device.

IMAGES OF ENGLAND

Standish & Shevington

Nicholas Webb
and staff of
Wigan Heritage Services

NONSUCH

Crooke pier, Shevington township, from Crooke Bridge, 1920s (see p. 47). In the background is Woodcock Row, a long terrace of cottages demolished in the 1960s.

First published 1999
This new pocket edition 2006
Images unchanged from first edition

Nonsuch Publishing Limited
The Mill, Brimscombe Port,
Stroud, Gloucestershire, GL5 2QG
www.nonsuch-publishing.com

Nonsuch Publishing is an imprint of Tempus Publishing Group

British Library Cataloguing in Publication Data.
A catalogue record for this book is available from the British Library.

ISBN 1-84588-321-7

Typesetting and origination by Nonsuch Publishing Limited
Printed in Great Britain by Oaklands Book Services Limited

Contents

Household goods and ffurniture

In the Brew house

	£	s	d
One large Iron Brewing pan and large Brass Cock and Iron Furnace	12	12	0
One Lead under bock and Lead pump fifty two foot	4	0	0
a Lead Cooler and Frame	5	0	0
Two large Mashing Tubbs	1	10	0
One Smaller Do.	0	8	0
Two Taking Tubbs	0	10	0
One lost Tubb	0	1	0
One Tunn Dish and Laiding piggen	0	1	6
Three pails	0	4	0
a Fire Shovel Tongs and Cowlrake	0	2	0
Two Dripers and three Troughs	0	3	6
a Lead Boiler with Copper Bottom and Iron Furnace	2	2	0

In the small beer Cellar

	£	s	d
Eight half Hogsheads at 3/ ϕ and four Hogsheads at 4:6 and two Stillages	2	3	0

In the Ale Cellar

	£	s	d
Four Hogsheads with broad hoops at 7/ ϕ	1	8	0
Three Do. at 3:6 ϕ	0	10	6
Three Wine pipes at 5/ ϕ	0	15	0
One half Hogshead	0	2	6
Four Stillages	0	6	0
One Oak Bottle Rack	1	10	0
Computed to be about two hundred Dozen of Bottles in Several parts of the House Quarts and pints at 2/ ϕ Dozen	20	0	0

In the men Servants Room

	£	s	d
An old Grate and Shovel at 8/ the Bed Stocks with green Hangings at 10/	0	10	8
a Feather Bed and Bolster weight 86 at 6 ϕ	2	3	0
Three large Blankets and a under one at 7/ a blew Quilt at 4/	0	11	0
Four Oak chairs at 4:6 ϕ and a old Arm Chair at 8/	0	18	8
The Bed Stocks with blew and white hangings	0	12	6
The Feather Bed and Bolster weight 60 at 5/ ϕ	1	5	0
Four old blankets at 3:6 a blew Quilt at 7:6 and two old Window Curtains 8/	0	11	8
Carried forward	60	01	6

A page from a detailed inventory of the contents of Standish Hall made in 1756 after the death of Ralph Standish, the last of the direct male line. There were estimated to be 2,400 beer or wine bottles in the house (Standish family papers).

Introduction

This is the fourth volume of the Archive Photographs series exploring the Wigan Metropolitan area, the others being *Around Leigh, Around Ashton and Golborne* and *Around Hindley and Abram*. Like the previous titles, *Around Standish and Shevington* has been compiled from the photographic collections of Wigan Heritage Service. These have been built up over many years to form one of the best local historical series in the north west. Most of the images originate from private collections - either donated or loaned for copying.

Although the Standish area has received much attention by historians (notably in T.C. Porteus' *History of the Parish of Standish, 1927*), this is the most comprehensive photographic history to have appeared. The area included is the southern part of the ancient parish, comprising the townships of Standish-with-Langtree, Shevington and Worthington, with one or two images from adjoining places. The Standish area has strong links with Wigan - political, religious, social and economic - but also has a fascinating history of its own. Until recent times Standish and Shevington were essentially villages, with rural features such as the country church and schools, a farming landscape, small village centres and scattered hamlets, and a few large houses with resident squires. At the first census in 1801 Standish had 1,500 inhabitants, Shevington only 646. The old Wigan borough, by comparison, had a population of 11,000.

The nineteenth century wrought tremendous change to the villages, here as elsewhere, and being in the Wigan coalfield meant that Standish and Shevington became industrial villages. Farming remained a part of the economy and social structure, but was displaced by coalmining and its associated trades. Coal was part of the local economy from medieval times, the earliest documented reference to mining rights being in a deed of 1350 where 'secole' (ordinary coal) and 'fyrston' (cannel) were specified. Mining reached the peak of its importance around 1914. The names of pits still live in local memories: Prospect, Swire, Victoria, Langtree, Broomfield, Taylor, John, Giant's Hall, in Standish, and Greenslate, Calico, Victoria & Albert in Shevington.

Associated with mining was the coming of new transport. The Douglas Navigation from the 1740s and the Leeds Liverpool Canal from 1781 left a decisive mark in Shevington, and Crooke became known mainly as a coal wharf. Other factories sprang up along the canal - paint, glue, brick making and stone quarrying.

Domestic weaving, which had flourished in the old cottages, was displaced by factory working. Other industries, local and further afield, affected employment patterns, and as the population grew, so shops and services expanded too. By 1901 Standish had over 7,000 people, Shevington nearly 2,000. Worthington, by contrast, remained a small rural township of only 233 people. Meanwhile industrial neighbouring Wigan had become the centre of a major parish of 150,000 souls.

What sort of place was Standish during the period covered by most of the images in this book? Firstly, it was an area where power and influence were held by an uneasy combination of old and new forces. The gentry still owned most of the land, as they had for hundreds of years. The Standish family were resident at Standish Hall up to the early 1800s. They had dominated the district as improving landlords, leaders of the Catholic congregation after the Reformation, and as early developers of the coal reserves beneath their estates. They still owned most of Standish and a large portion of Shevington up to World War I. Charles Strickland Standish was elected MP for Wigan in 1837 and 1842 and was buried in the family vault at St Wilfrid's in 1863.

However, the agricultural depression that blighted England from the 1870s onwards, the family's increasing residence on the continent from the 1820s and the rapid development of the mines, fossilised the estate. Like many estates elsewhere after the Settled Land Acts were passed (1882-90), it was finally broken up at sales in 1912 and 1921. This had a dramatic effect on Standish, suddenly making available building land for the suburbanization of the area which has been an inexorable process from the 1920s onwards. Semi-detached villas, council houses and the many private estates built since 1950 increased the population to 11,000 by 1971 (the last figure for the old Urban District), despite a serious decline in heavy industry during the same period.

Similar change occurred in Shevington where the land, which was divided between smaller estates, was even more rapidly built over. By 1971 (when Shevington was in Wigan Rural District), the population had reached 8,000, and is now around 13,000.

Social and political power at the end of the nineteenth and the beginning of the twentieth centuries was also exercised by the Church, in the person of the rector Charles Hutton who also managed a large estate, and by the new local councils. Standish became a Local Board in 1872 and an Urban District in 1894, other services being provided by the County Council. Since 1974 Standish and Shevington have been part of a large unitary authority, Wigan Metropolitan Borough.

Economic, political and social power was also wielded by the 'new men' of the area - industrialists who developed the mines and factories, and professional and business men. Most people in 1900 lived their lives by the harsh demands of these entrepreneurs, working long hours for low wages in dangerous conditions, with poor housing and health provision, and only the friendly societies and Poor Law Guardians as safety nets. Meanwhile the *nouveaux riches* aped the habits of the gentry, either building imitation country houses (e.g. Kilhey Court, The Beeches, The Limes, Ashfield House, Shevington Hall), or renting the genuine article; Standish Hall itself was occupied variously in the nineteenth century by mill owners Thomas Darwell and Nathaniel Eckersley and finally by J.B. Almond of Almond's brewery.

With industry came blight, which affected the villages quite seriously. In 1865 the agent to the Standish estate reported that the timber and hedges were moribund due to the poisonous air from factory chimneys. The opening of Victoria Colliery in 1900 by Lord Crawford's Wigan Coal & Iron Co. marked the high point of local industry. Decline was rapid after the First World War and the last pit at Robin Hill closed in 1963. The Wigan district was badly afflicted by the inter-war depression, and Standish and Shevington shared in this economic blizzard. But the images in this book show above all a community spirit in such festivals as walking days, sport and family events, and a pride in village life, despite hard times, which is the legacy inherited by the new post-industrial community.

One

Around the Villages

Horrocks' Ford Bridge, which carries Red Rock Lane over the river Douglas, bears an inscription marking one of Lancashire's medieval divisions. Counties were divided into 'hundreds'; Standish fell within Leyland hundred. The hundreds had their own courts, and were still used as administrative units into the present century. In the Second World War such inscriptions were painted out in case of enemy invasion. Several years later the inscription was still partially defaced; looking on is Tom Banks. The present bridge dates from the rebuilding of 1882, although the iron work is date stamped 1842.

A silvan idyll: Beech Walk, Standish, c. 1910.

The stone cross at the north end of Beech Walk. This is a modern replica, but the sites and pedestals of ancient crosses are recorded on Green Lane and Standish Wood Lane by the Ordnance Survey, and three bases are preserved today as ancient monuments. Their original purpose is likely to have been as boundary markers for the estate granted in Langtree to Cockersand Abbey, c. 1220.

Above: 'Spite Row' (nos. 7-16 Market Place), prior to demolition in 1930. Legend has it that these houses were originally built by the Catholic Standishes to block the view of the parish church. By their style they were built in the early 1800s and probably incorporated weaving rooms.

Right: The cross in Standish Market Place, early 1900s. The base is reckoned to be medieval, the present cross being of eighteenth-century style. There was probably a local customary market here. An annual fair for horses, cattle and toys was formerly held on St Cecilia's Day (22 November), possibly established by or in memory of Cecilia Standish, lord of the manor between 1755 and 1778.

Market Place, early 1900s. To the left of the cross is the original village well, guarded by railings and lit by gas, which had been superseded by the arrival of piped water in 1892. Behind is Amos Allen's florist and greengrocer's shop, which occupied nos. 2 and 3 Market Place from the 1890s to the 1930s.

A snow scene in Standish Market Place, c. 1914.

Market Place, 1930s. In 1930 Spite Row was demolished to open up the view of the church, and the well was covered by a canopy. The work was paid for by James Ainscough, a Standish farm boy who rose from humble beginnings to become head of Pendlebury's department store and in 1922 mayor of Wigan. The 'Peace Gate' (right) had been erected in 1926 as a church war memorial; it contains a statue of St Wilfrid.

Market Place, c. 1950. During the Second World War the well was identified as an emergency water supply by the National Fire Service, but in 1943 the canopy, after only a few years standing, was demolished accidentally by an American service vehicle. Subsequently the well was sealed. In 1998 a replacement canopy was erected following archaeological excavation of the well.

Above: The stocks, a traditional means of public humiliation for minor offenders in England, were apparently found in a field and brought to the Market Place, in about 1900, replacing a large tree shown on the 1892 Ordnance Survey map. Since then they have been a favourite with photographers. The name of this victim is unknown.

Left: Tom Hughes (bottom right) the renowned Lancashire cyclist, photographed in 1934.

STANDISH STOCKS & MARKET CROSS,
4 MILES FROM WIGAN PIER. (4.7.34)

Market Street, c. 1920. This crossroads was the northern terminus of Wigan Corporation's tram system. Williams Deacon's Bank occupied the first property on High Street.

Market Street, c. 1960. Although less busy than today, cars have replaced trams, controlled by the first traffic lights. Spite Row has gone, and Noel Chadwick's shop has opened at the corner of Preston Road, part of a long-established butchery and one of Standish's most successful modern businesses.

School Lane, *c.* 1914. This view gives a good impression of the growth of Victorian Standish. On the right are small cottages of the early 1800s, inhabited by weavers and colliers. Half-way down is the Dog & Partridge beer house. On the left are bay-window terraces of about 1895 built by the brewer J.B. Almond (who lived at The Beeches), leading down to Almonds brewery itself; in front of the brewery School Lane was crossed by a mineral railway serving local collieries.

High Street, *c.* 1914, looking south past Cross Street corner, showing a variety of eighteenth- and nineteenth-century cottage types. Two shops can be seen: John Howard, butcher (centre left) and Joseph Hooson, clogger (centre-right), one of a family of cloggers who used locally grown wood. The block in the centre was later demolished to make way for the Palace Cinema, which in turn was demolished after closure in 1956.

Church Street, c. 1950. The terrace on the left is mid-Victorian. The extensive Black Horse Hotel or Inn was one of six pubs and two beer houses in Standish owned by Almonds brewery; originally it was the Glebe Inn, part of the large estate belonging to the rectors.

Wigan Road, looking north September 1950. This view shows the inter-war ribbon development of Standish towards Wigan, following the sale of the Standish Hall estate in 1921. The suburban semi-detached villas on the left, built around 1930 with names such as Moat House and Beech View, are in marked contrast to the Victorian rows beyond. Until the 1920s Wigan Road was open farmland as far as the Boar's Head.

High Street, c. 1920. 'Car Terminus' refers to the electric tram terminus. The Wheat Sheaf Hotel at the crossroads was another Almond's pub; Arthur Naylor, whose name can be seen on the sign board, took over the licence in 1914. The large shop at the corner of Pole Street (centreright) was a branch of the Wigan grocer O. & G. Rushton; the late TV personality William Rushton was a member of this family.

Broad o'th' Lane, Shevington, c. 1910. Unlike Standish, Shevington was a scattered township of hamlets and farms, but this was the nearest thing to a village centre, with the Plough & Harrow pub (Sumner's brewery), shop (centre-left), finger-post and, just off the picture (left), St Anne's church.

Above: Gathurst Lane, June 1904. These old cottages north of Gathurst Bridge, together with a few farms and larger houses, formed another of Shevington's hamlets; Gathurst south of the Douglas lay within Orrell township. The cottage at the far end was the post office (see p. 106).

Right: Worthington and Shevington sections of Worrall's Wigan Directory, 1869. Farming was still a major economic activity in these townships, but coal mining was already important.

WORTHINGTON.

Ainsworth Henry, farmer
Alker William, blacksmith
Dicconson James, wheelwright
Dicconson Thomas, farmer
Hampson John, farmer
Hampson Mary, farmer
Hampson Robert, farmer
Mort Mary, farmer

Ollerton, Jane, farmer
Ollerton Peter, farmer
Silvester Edward, Esq., J.P., North hall
Watkinson John, farmer, The Hall

—
***Letters are received through Wigan

SHEVINGTON.

Atherton John, *Navigation Inn*, Gathurst bridge
Barton Mrs., shopkeeper
Brindle William, *Hesketh Arms*
Cooper Peter, beer retailer
Danson Robert, farmer
Hilton Margaret, farmer
Hilton Thomas, farmer
Hindley E., day school, Crook
Horrocks Thomas, shopkeeper
Lang W. E. farmer
Mann G. W., colliery manager
Marsh and Co., coal proprietors, Green Slate colliery; John Redshaw, manager
Marsh Richard, beer retailer
Martland James, farmer
Orrell James, farmer

Park Richard, farmer
Ratcliffe John, blacksmith
Richardson Rev. A.
Redshaw John, colliery manager
Shuffleton Joseph, farmer, Crook hall
Stopford Richard, *Plough & Harrow Inn*
Tayleur John & Co., coal proprietors, Shevington colliery; G. W. Mann, manager
Tyrer John, *Crook Hall Inn*
Wilding Edward, beer retailer
Woods Hugh, farmer

National School; John Basnett, master
National School, Crook

Above: View near John Colliery. Several photographs survive from the early 1900s to illustrate Standish's essentially rural nature at that time.

Left: Fields and woods near Standish Hall, early 1900s.

Two

The Standish Family

Standish Hall, the ancestral home of the lords of the manor of Standish. This pen and ink drawing of 1897 by Fred Barnish shows the Tudor wing (centre) and Roman Catholic chapel (right) which was rebuilt in the 1740s.

Ordnance Survey map (1894) showing the position of Standish Hall relative to the village. It is likely that the original manor house was located closer to the church. By 1921, when it was auctioned, the estate extended to some 3,000 acres. In the 1930s the Park was used as a golf course.

Standish Hall: approach from the south-west, *c.* 1910. The hall was apparently moated until about 1780 when the demesne was laid out as a landscape park in the 'Capability Brown' style. Hall Farm can be seen to the right of picture.

Old drawing room, Standish Hall: one of only two interior photographs known to have survived. The panelling and ceiling are Jacobean in style, while the carved overmantels came from Borwick Hall near Carnforth, following the marriage of William Standish to Cecilia Bindloss of Borwick in 1660; the arms are (left) the Stuart kings and (right) Bindloss.

JamesR

JAMES the Second by the grace of God King of England Scotland France and Ireland defender of the Faith &c. To Our Trusty and well beloved

Greeting. This is to autorize you to raife and command a Regiment of Horfe in *England* for our Service and to obey the orders from time to time according to the Difciplin of war. Given at Our Court at St. Germains the *twentieth* day of *June 1692* And in the *eighth* year of Our Reigne.

By his Majeftys Comand.

meltest

A blank commission issued by the exiled James II in France, 20 June 1692. One of a series preserved amongst the Standish family papers, together with letters in code and invisible ink. After James' deposition in 1688 Catholic families such as the Standishes plotted to restore him (and later his son) to the throne. Discovery of the 'Standish Plot' led the conspirators being tried in 1694. Standish Hall was searched but the accused were acquitted for lack of evidence.

By the King,
A PROCLAMATION,

For Apprehending of *William Standish* of *Standish-Hall* in the
County of *Lancaster*, Esquire.

WILLIAM R.

Hereas His Majesty hath received Information, That William Standish of Standish-Hall in the County of Lancaster, Esquire, hath Conspired, with divers other Disaffected Persons, to Disturb and Destroy the Government, and for that purpose bought up Arms, and Abetted and Adhered to His Majesties Enemies; For which cause several Warrants have Issued for the Apprehending of the said William Standish, but he hath withdrawn himself from his usual Place of Abode, and is fled from Justice: His Majesty therefore hath thought fit, by and with the Advice of His Privy Council, and upon an Humble Address from the House of Commons for that purpose, to Issue this His Royal Proclamation; And His Majesty doth hereby Command and Require all His Loving Subjects to Discover, Take and Apprehend the said William Standish Wheresoever he may be found, and to Carry him before the next Justice of Peace, or Chief Magistrate, who is hereby Required to Commit him to the next Gaol, there to remain until he be thence delivered by due Course of Law. And His Majesty doth Require the said Justice, or other Magistrate immediately to give Notice thereof to His Privy Council, or one of the Principal Secretaries of State. And His Majesty doth hereby Publish and Declare, That all Persons who shall Conceal the said William Standish, or be Aiding or Assisting in Concealing him, or furthering his Escape, shall be Proceeded against for such their Offence, with the utmost Severity according to Law. And His Majesty does hereby Promise, That whosoever shall Discover and Apprehend the said William Standish, and Bring him before some Justice of Peace, or Chief Magistrate, shall Have and Receive the Reward of Five hundred Pounds for so doing. And We do hereby Authorize and Require Our present Commissioners of Our Treasury, and Our high Treasurer and Commissioners of Our Treasury for the time being, to make Payment of the said Sum accordingly.

Given at Our Court at *Kensington* the Fourteenth Day of *March* 1694. In the Seventh Year of Our Reign.

God save the King.

London, Printed by *Charles Bill*, and the Executrix of *Thomas Newcomb* deceas'd, Printers to the Kings most Excellent Majesty. 1694.

A royal proclamation for the arrest of William Standish, 1694, offering a reward of £500 for his apprehension. He was accused of conspiring 'with divers other disaffected persons, to disturb and destroy the government'. William Dicconson of Wrightington Hall and Sir William Gerard were arrested, but Standish escaped. Protestant William of Orange had replaced James (whose daughter Mary he had married) to become William III in 1689.

Above: Design for the 'chimney-side section of the dining room', Standish Hall, by Joseph Bonomi, 1782. This Adam-style design was probably never executed, but may have been prepared for Edward Standish, who inherited the estate in 1778. It is typical of new country-house interiors of the period. Bonomi was an Italian architect who settled in England; he also prepared a design for Edward's brother Charles at Towneley Hall.

Left: A seventeenth-century door and panelling in one of the upper rooms of Standish Hall, photographed for the estate sale catalogue, 1921. It is believed that panelling and a plaster ceiling removed after the sale were used to refurbish Halsway Manor, Somerset, which is now a centre for the study of folk culture.

Standish Hall from the south, *c.* 1910.

Standish Hall from the south: an engraving of 1828. The Hall was an interesting mixture of periods and styles: the central brick block of 1748, connected to the chapel by a wing surviving from the rebuilding of about 1574 and, to the left, a single storey wing containing new dining and drawing rooms built in 1822.

The lodge house and gate at the top of Beech Walk, early 1900s, in a broken glass plate photograph. Dating probably from the improvements to the Hall and estate carried out around 1800, this lodge guarded the main drive to the Hall; the keeper in 1914 was Edward Hilton. After the sale of 1921 (when it was the lodge to Strickland House), the house became a private residence, and today is a listed building.

Standish Hall, September 1950. When the estate was auctioned at Empress Hall, Wigan in March 1921, the Hall was withdrawn at £4,800. Subsequently it was reported that the Tudor wing and chapel were dismantled and shipped to America; recent efforts to locate their whereabouts have proved fruitless. The remainder was partly demolished and adapted to form two smaller houses, seen here; these in turn were knocked down in the early 1980s.

Three

At Home

Crooke Hall, *c.* 1900. Built in 1608 for Peter Catterall and his wife Elizabeth, the house overlooked the River Douglas, and latterly the canal. Subsidence and consequent flooding led to Crooke Hall's demolition in 1937. A timber panel, carved with the initials of Peter, Elizabeth and the original carpenters, and with crude portraits of the former, is on display at The History Shop in Wigan.

Worthington Hall, c. 1900. The manor of Worthington was held by a family of that name from before 1212 up to the late 1600s. Built in 1577 by Edward Worthington it was subsequently altered in stone and brick, and only the central section of the black and white work shown here can be seen today.

Main door of Worthington Hall, showing the carved name of Edward Worthington and date, 1577, together with the initials M.O. (perhaps the carpenter) in the left spandrel.

Right: Shevington Old Hall, *c.* 1920. Situated off Miles Lane near Broad o'th' Lane, the hall was built probably by the Woodward family in the seventeenth century. Shevington manor was divided at an early date, and the Woodwards held the estate of the Rigbys, lords of Leyland. The hall was demolished in 1961.

Below: 'Manor House', Gathurst Lane, Shevington, an unusual Tudor style house, photographed shortly before demolition in 1961.

'Manor House', Worthington in the 1950s, a seventeenth-century building originally known as Worthington Mill House, opposite Standish Bleach Works on Chorley Road. This was a small estate, the centre of which was part of the endowment of the Holy Rood chantry in Standish parish church, founded in 1483. After the Dissolution it was acquired by Edward Standish and remained part of the Standish estate. In the early 1900s it was used partly as a sub-post office.

Giant's Hall, Standish Wood Lane, 1988, takes its name from the boulders nearby (probably glacial), which, according to local legend, were thrown there by a giant. The date stone reads 'WPL 1673', referring to William Lathom who died in 1691.

Finch House off Miles Lane, Shevington, c. 1900. Between 1741 and 1752 this imposing house was the residence of Edward Dicconson, the Roman Catholic Vicar General of the Northern District. He was one of the Dicconsons of Wrightington Hall, whose estate included much property in Shevington; a memorial tablet to him can be seen in Standish parish church.

Bradley Hall, Standish, 1988. Probably medieval in origin with a Georgian brick facade and Gothick gables, Bradley Hall was part of a small estate owned by various families over the centuries; a coloured estate plan of 1765 shows its extent. During the Second World War an ammunition factory was built nearby, and after the war Heinz had a factory on the site of Hall Farm. In recent years the house has been a night club and commercial offices.

Bogburn Hall, *c.* 1920. Situated in Coppull township to the north of Standish village, Bogburn was built in 1663 by Roger and Alice Haydock and was a centre for early Quaker meetings.

Arley Hall, a postcard from the early 1900s. Situated just beyond the parish boundary in Blackrod, Arley (like Standish and Bradley) was originally a moated medieval house. Overlooking the Leeds-Liverpool Canal at Red Rock, it has some fine Georgian Gothic features. It is now the home of Wigan Golf Club.

The Hermitage, near Beech Walk, early 1900s. An eighteenth-century house provided by the Standish family for Catholic priests serving their chapel and the local congregation, The Hermitage became the first presbytery for St Marie's R.C. church when the latter was built in 1884. In 1908 it was replaced by the new presbytery, and was demolished in the 1970s.

Shevington (New) Hall, c. 1930s. A small Victorian country house on the site of an earlier property, this is recalled today by older residents as 'the big house' of the village in the early years of the twentieth century. Home of local coal owner John Tayleur from about 1840 to 1876, it was later occupied by Theobald Dixon (see p. 124). It stood near the present Hall Close.

Standish Rectory, Rectory Lane, after enlargement by Revd Charles Hutton in 1887. A substantial country house with lodge, coach house, stables and greenhouses, The Rectory was also the centre of a glebe estate of some 270 acres providing a living worth £1,200 p.a. The house became important in village social life during Hutton's incumbency. Largely demolished after his retirement in 1937, outbuildings were converted in recent years into The Owls restaurant.

Club House Farm, Shevington, early 1900s. Situated at the sharp bend where Wigan Lower Road meets Church Lane, this farm was part of the Standish estate. A date stone in the old barn bears the date 1660, and a window in the house is etched with the date 1663. When the estate was auctioned in 1921 the sitting tenant Harry Hilton bought the freehold.

Highfield Farm, Gathurst Lane, Shevington, stood near the present Highfield Avenue. A small farm of 29 acres, this too was a tenancy of the Standish estate.

Mill Dam House, Shevington, c. 1900. Standish Hall corn mill was powered by Mill Brook, and stood at the end of Parkbrook Lane. There was probably a manorial mill on the site since the fourteenth century. A dam behind the mill created a sufficient head of water.

Above: Cat i'th' Window cottage, Almond Brook Road, Standish, shortly before destruction by fire in 1901. The silhouette cats in the blank windows are said to be successors of plaster cats originally used to advertise the presence of a priest during the Catholic persecution. A more prosaic explanation is that they were a dairyman's sign.

Left: Cat 'th' Window cottage after rebuilding, with the cats repainted.

The Lodge, Wigan Road, Standish, c. 1920. Guarding the entrance to Prospect Hill House (built 1793), and beyond that to Standish Hall, the lodge is one of Standish's many listed buildings. Prospect was occupied by James Ainscough, local philanthropist and chairman of Pendlebury's (see p. 13), and is now used as a nursing home.

'Garden Villas', at the corner of Preston Road and Pepper Lane, c. 1920. Ten houses built as model cottages in the garden suburb style by E.H. Monks, a local businessman, builder and experimental farmer. This type of housing was quite revolutionary for a mining village such as Standish.

New council houses at Fairhurst Avenue, Standish, 1920s. In October 1920 Standish UDC began to build 133 houses to Ministry of Health standards. Each contained a living room, scullery, pantry, coal house, inside toilet, three bedrooms and bathroom; some had a parlour too. Owing to central government economies, the scheme was halted when Fairhurst Avenue was completed, an early example of excellent municipal housing.

New bungalows in Standish, 1960s. Small towns and villages such as Standish and Shevington experienced a boom in private house building from the 1950s onwards. 'Bungalow' was a word applied to a superior rest house for colonial administrators in India, but was adopted at home to distinguish these new houses from older single-storey labourers' dwellings.

Four

At Work

The Finch family working their land at Robin Hill farm off Pepper Lane, Standish, early 1900s.

Left: The Ball family at Naylor's farm off Miles Lane, Shevington, *c.* 1918. Naylor's is now the lodge for Gathurst Golf Club, overlooking the M6 motorway. Mr Ball seems to be cutting faggots.

Below: Working with steam power at Naylor's farm, Shevington, *c.* 1914.

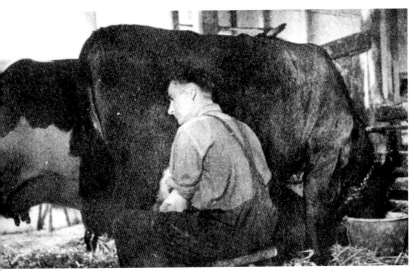

Milking by hand at Brown's farm, Standish Wood Folds, *c.* 1935. The farm was occupied during the 1920s and 30s by Thomas Hilton.

Basket makers at Shevington: a rare photograph of about 1897. Basket weaving was a domestic craft still practised in the twentieth century using locally grown willow or alder shoots.

Worthington paper mills, late nineteenth century, by John Cooper of Wigan. A water-powered mill on the Douglas existed here from at least the 1300s. The Cromptons operated a paper mill here from the late 1700s and by 1840 a steam engine had been installed. Paper making ceased in 1883.

Worthington bleach works, early 1900s. The paper mill was taken over in 1884 by Taylor & Co. as a bleach factory for the local cotton industry. Dyeing was added to the process and bleaching ceased in 1907, by which time the business was known as the Standish Company. Textile finishing continued until 1998 when the factory was closed by Carrington Viyella.

Aerial view of Worthington bleach works and reservoirs, c. 1930. The reservoirs were built between 1855 and 1872 by the newly established Wigan Corporation Water Works which had taken over the water company that supplied the town from 1764. The river Douglas was culverted beneath the reservoirs and the factory. The area is now popular for recreation under the name Worthington Lakes.

Aerial view of Roburite factory and Gathurst station, c. 1920. Roburite, an explosive patented by Dr Carl Roth, was produced here from 1888. The factory had its own narrow gauge railway across the Douglas Valley and a wharf on the canal (right). A Wigan bound train passes the sidings whence the products were despatched to mines and quarries around Britain.

Left: Wrapping an explosives cartridge at the Roburite works, *c.* 1910. Normally the worker would have worn protective clothing (see below).

Below: Women workers of the Roburite Explosives Company, *c.* 1923. The toxic nature of chemicals used in the process made protective clothing essential.

Crooke pier, 1890s, by Revd William Wickham, a notable Wigan photographer. 'Pier' (as in Wigan Pier) in this sense denotes a coal wagon tippler, where barges were loaded for delivery to Liverpool and other towns. Crooke pier was built in 1859 to serve Standish & Shevington Cannel Co.'s John Pit and was connected also to Kirkless Hall Coal & Iron Co.'s railway.

Chimney of Prince Albert Colliery, Shevington, 1920s, looking along Shevington Lane at the junction with Church Lane. The pit was part of John Tayleur's Shevington Colliery, developed to exploit the Arley Mine seam at a depth of 245 yards. Tayleur's ('Tillywers' to the locals) was taken over by Wigan Coal & Iron Co. in 1876 and closed in 1877; the chimney stood until 1927.

Sinking the shaft at Wigan Coal & Iron Co.'s Victoria Colliery, Standish in 1900, a rare photograph of this operation which began on 15 May. Situated on the west side of the London-Glasgow main line, between Standish and Boar's Head, this was the last big colliery to be opened in the Wigan coalfield.

Victoria Colliery: screens under construction, c. 1900. Note the impressive double winding engine house, with headgear at either end. Victoria was nationalised in 1947 with the other pits of Wigan Coal Corporation. It was closed in July 1958, but the engine house survived until 1990.

Screening at Victoria Colliery, early 1900s. In Lancashire this was traditionally a female job. Coal was tipped onto shaking conveyor belts from which the women picked out stone and other waste.

Coal pickers at Broomfield Colliery, Standish, 1912. The national strike of 1912 lasted for six weeks, over the issue of a minimum wage for underground workers. Hardship caused by the strike led to miners and their families scouring waste heaps for small pieces of coal for use or sale. Broomfield employed over 200 workers around this time.

Giants Hall Colliery, 1930s. Developed by Wigan Coal & Iron Co. between 1875 and 1881 on the site of the former William pit, abandoned in the 1840s, Giants Hall tapped the cannel and Arley seams. Nationalised in 1947 it was closed in 1961.

John Pit, Standish Lower Ground, 1948. Sunk originally in 1836 and abandoned soon after, it was re-opened by Standish & Shevington Cannel Co. in 1858. Passing eventually to Wigan Coal & Iron Co. (which became Wigan Coal Corporation in 1930), John was closed in April 1954.

Chisnall Hall Colliery during modernization by the National Coal Board, September 1947. Just inside Coppull township, Chisnall was developed by Pearson & Knowles' Coal & Iron Co. between 1891 and 1900. The steelwork of a new pit bank and headgear can be seen, enclosing the original timber structure. The colliery closed in March 1967.

Welch Whittle Colliery, shortly before closure in February 1960. Sunk by the Blainscough Colliery Co. between 1892 and 1894, it succeeded an earlier pit on the same site. Welch Whittle was the smallest township in Standish parish by population.

Workers at 'the bone hole', Shevington, 1909. This was a glue factory overlooking the Leeds
-Liverpool Canal, whose raw material, animal bones, caused a notorious stench. Operated by
Grove Chemical Co. as Crown Glue Works, it succeeded an earlier paint factory built in 1850
by Charles Scarisbrick of Wrightington Hall. The glue works closed in 1980, but its extent can
still be traced on the ground.

Logitek Distribution plant, Bradley industrial estate, c. 1980. With the decline of heavy industry,
continued local employment has depended upon new technology. Since 1979 Logitek has
supplied computer systems from Standish and has expanded rapidly in personnel and premises.

Five

At School

Former parish school building, Rectory Lane, early 1900s, which also housed the Sunday school from 1829. In the 1790s the rector's niece Mary Smalley founded a 'School of Pious Learning and Useful Industry' for twenty girls who were taught needlework, spinning and knitting. This was absorbed in the 1820s by the new National School, predecessor of the present C. of E. School, which occupied this building until the 1960s.

Standish C. of E. infants' school, 1st class, 1922. Infants were housed on the ground floor (see p. 53), and the girls on the first floor.

Standish Grammar School boys, 1898-99. During this period at least half the boys went to work in the coal mines on leaving; others to the bleach works or to local tradesmen. Established under the will of Mary Langton (d. 1604), the school taught 'grammar' for up to 40 fee paying boys. Practically defunct by 1853, it was refounded in 1861 as a village elementary school, with over 230 boys by 1900.

Above: Standish Grammar School, early 1900s. Built at School Croft, near the corner of Green Lane and School Lane, this site continued in use until 1964, by which time the school had become part of Standish C. of E. School and the first part of the present St. Wilfrid's had been built on Rectory Lane. The old grammar school was demolished in 1968 and the site is now occupied by Greenacres Home.

Right: An advertisement from Wigan Directory (1869) for Miss Masters' private school. South Villa stood where Moss Grove stands today. Like many private schools this was short-lived. Others were Miss Howard's above the council offices, Miss Thompson's in Cross Street, Miss Thorburn's in High Street, and even a room in the Eagle & Child pub was used for a time. Sarah Masters, daughter of an auctioneer from Coventry, was keeping house for her brother in Wigan by 1881.

Left: Pupils of Crooke school with their walking day banner, 1930s. Opened in 1872 by the newly established Shevington School Board under the 1870 Education Act, Crooke flourished as a village school until its closure in 1985. The building still stands, adjoining the Methodist chapel. It replaced an earlier mission school near the Canal tunnel (see p.65).

Below: Music time at Crooke school, 1930s, one of a series of official photographs illustrating current teaching methods. Introducing children to music through simple instruments like this was still being practised in the 1970s. Note the wind-up gramophone!

Hands up! This is either an exercise class or a general punishment to find out who broke a window.

Milk time. Few people over thirty will forget the experience of school milk, nicely warmed by the sun, drunk through a straw from the bottle. Older readers will recognise the wide-necked bottles of the period.

Cheerful faces at Crooke village school, 1930s.

Playtime at Crooke school, 1978. Falling rolls led to closure seven years later.

Broad o'th' Lane School, Shevington, 1970s. Opened in 1814 as a 'school for pious and useful learning' with the aid of public subscriptions, the founder was 'R.P.R.', almost certainly 'Richard Perryn, Rector' of Standish (1779 - 1826), who founded a similar school at Adlington. The original block (centre) is still used. Like Crooke school, it came under the Shevington School Board in 1870 and was subsequently extended.

SHEVINGTON. NEW COUNCIL SCHOOL

Additions to Broad o'th' Lane school, 1927. These further extensions by Lancashire County Education Committee reflect the growth of elementary education and the higher leaving age of 14 introduced in 1921. Primary schools such as Shevington in effect developed senior departments, with five new classrooms and an assembly hall, designed on the fashionable principles of natural light and ventilation.

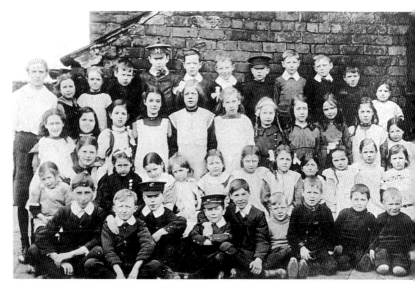

A mixed class at Shevington Council School, Broad o'th' Lane, 1914. The boys with the Eton collars may have been prefects or monitors, and the one with the 'H' cap perhaps head boy.

Senior school drama production at Broad o'th' Lane, 1936, probably *Pirates of Penzance* .

Mixed class at Shevington Council School, 1955.

Pupils from Shevington Junior School, Broad o'th' Lane, on their trip to Knocke, Belgium, 1959, a treat beyond the imagination of the class of 1914. Headmaster Tom Holding is on the right.

Elsie and Connie Cooksey, teachers at St Anne's Sunday school, Shevington, early 1900s. The Sunday school movement was started in 1780 by Robert Raikes in Gloucester, with the aim of giving children a grounding in scripture and religious instruction. Until well into the 1800s it remained the only form of schooling for many children. By 1900 it had become an addition to Sunday service.

Boys classes at Coppull Moor C. of E. School, 1923. Coppull was one of the ten townships of Standish parish, and was the first to have its own chapelry licensed for worship. It had its first church school in 1846, and Coppull Moor (near Chisnall Hall colliery), was opened in 1874.

Six

At Prayer

Standish parish church: an eighteenth-century painting. The main body of the church dates from the rebuilding of the 1580s, detailed accounts for which survive. Robert Charnock was in charge of the work, Laurence Shipway being master mason. The spire shown here was blown down in 1822 and both spire and tower rebuilt in 1867. The painting also shows (left) 'Spite Row' (see p. 11).

Standish parish church, in about 1870, showing the new steeple.

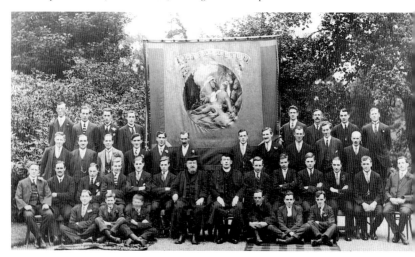

Senior men's bible class, St Wilfrid's, 1899. Church societies, including bible study groups, were important aspects of parish life in the late 1800s and early 1900s.

Right: Revd C.W.N. Hutton (Rector 1886-1937) and sister Marion, probably at his retirement in 1936. Hutton made many additions to the church and rectory, and was at the centre of village social life. His hobbies were cricket and collecting mezzotints, on which he became an authority. He also had business and financial interests.

Below: Crooke school and mission church shortly before demolition, late 1800s. Built in 1845 as a school, it was licensed for worship in 1855 and baptisms registered there until 1863. The buildings became unusable due to flooding and Crooke had to wait until Shevington was assigned an ecclesiastical district, and St Anne's opened in 1887, for the Church of England to have a closer presence than the mother church at Standish.

Chancel screen in St Anne's church, Shevington, possibly at the time of its consecration in 1896. Its merits were for a long time a matter of controversy, and it was finally removed in 1959.

St Anne's church choir, 1950s.

Tunley Presbyterian chapel, 1983. Situated at Mossy Lea, just beyond the Standish boundary in Wrightington township, Tunley is the most significant nonconformist church in the area and one of the oldest foundations in Lancashire. Built in 1691 under the Act of Toleration by the Wilsons of South Tunley Hall, it has been in continuous use ever since.

The original Friends' Meeting House shortly before demolition in 1904. Situated on Preston Road near the Pepper Lane junction, it was built in 1717 next to a burial ground that was registered in 1693. In 1803 the Quakers moved to a new meeting house in School Lane (Quakers' Place), but ceased to meet by c. 1850. The burial ground can still be seen today, laid out as a small green.

Almond Brook Methodist Church
Chorley Circuit.

Silver Jubilee Celebrations
NOVEMBER 13th, 1935.
SERMON 4 p.m. PUBLIC TEA 5 p.m. MEETING 7 p.m.

Dear Friend,

We are preparing to celebrate the 25th Anniversary of the opening of our Church at Almond Brook, and we seek your co-operation in making it an outstanding success.

During the past 25 years we have experienced both trials and triumphs, and looking back we can truly say "*Hitherto hath the Lord helped us.*" We rejoice in the good congregations that gather for worship Sunday by Sunday and in the fine spiritual tone pervading our services. A reporter from the "*Chorley Guardian*" attending an ordinary service a few weeks ago was impressed by the homely atmosphere, the splendid singing, and the whole influence at the service.

We believe that with a growing population around us we have a Call from God to do even greater things in His name.

We feel that the best way of celebrating our Jubilee will be to raise enough money in order that our Church may be Renovated and Re-decorated, and to re-dedicate ourselves for a great Spiritual Advance in this neighbourhood.

Will YOU help us by your Prayers and your Gifts? We enclose an envelope so that you may share in these celebrations by giving a Jubilee Thank-offering for all the good you have received from this Church. (A small sum put aside every week would enable you to make a gift in November that is appropriate for such an occasion.)

Our financial aim is **£100.**

Yours in Christian service,

Rev. G. A. MALAND,
J. D. GRAY, Secretary,
A. TRAFFORD. Assist. Secretary,
ED. TURNER, Treasurer.

Above: Opening of Standish Wesleyan Methodist church, High Street, 13 July 1897. Methodist preachers were present in Standish in 1790, and by 1858 the Wesleyans had purchased the Quaker Meeting House in School Lane, and began a fund for the new church in 1885. Meanwhile the Primitives opened a new chapel on Preston Road in 1891.

Left: Appeal circular for Almond Brook Methodist church, 1935. Opened in 1910 with Sunday school adjoining, at Shevington Moor (formerly Crow Orchard Road), this was one of several Primitive chapels in the area, others being at Shevington Vale and Crooke. In 1932 the 'Prims' joined nationally with the Wesleyans and United Methodists, though Crooke church had been shared from as early as 1894.

St Marie's Roman Catholic church and presbytery, Standish, early 1900s. After the Reformation adherents of the 'old faith' had worshipped in secret, served by itinerant priests. As toleration grew, Standish Hall chapel was provided for the local community and served until the opening of St Marie's in 1884.

St Marie's RC church, c. 1900. The original wooden altar seen here was replaced by one of marble in 1923.

Above: Convent of Notre Dame, shortly after the new buildings were opened at Roundmoor Road, Standish, 1965. Founded in 1854 on Standishgate, Wigan, the convent retained its cloister design, the new building providing forty cells. The Sisters, whose mission is to care for children, continued to maintain a school at the old site until 1974.

Left: Haydock memorial tablet, Standish parish church, installed in 1922. This commemorates Lieutenant George Haydock of the US Air Force who was killed in the First World War, and other Haydock ancestors (see p.34). It was dedicated by a descendant of Robert (d. 1760) who emigrated to America about 1734.

Seven

Walking Days

Walking Day, Standish, *c*.1910. One of a series of photographs probably recording the same walk at various points of the route. Annual walking days seem to have been introduced by the Victorian clergy to replace the traditional rowdier wakes, held at the parish saints' days. The religious flavour is seen here in the banner 'Christ the Good Shepherd'. A likely location for this picture is Rectory Lane.

Passing the Wheatsheaf, Preston Road, heading towards High Street.

High Street, looking north from a point near the Wesleyan church. The awning of William Gray's shop can be seen (centre) and the Wheatsheaf pub (far left).

View of the parade from a point near no. 33, High Street; the cobbled lane at the left led to the original cricket ground. Note the tram lines running down the centre of the road, and the tarmac strips either side, no doubt to accommodate the growing volume of motor traffic along what soon became the busy A49. The banner was from St Wilfrid's.

Another view of Walking Day from the same point as above.

Left: The banner reaches the Market Place, watched by boys wearing their best Eton collars. Beyond can be seen Samuel Hale's grocery shop.

Below: Leaving Market Place and walking down Rectory Lane, no doubt with tea on their minds. Left is a typical Victorian lych-gate (erected, *c.* 1854); centre, the villas called Beckside and St Wilfrid's House (built, *c.* 1900) and beyond, the original parish school building, still used for the infants up to the 1960s.

Walkers take their ease on the lawns at the rectory, where refreshments were provided.

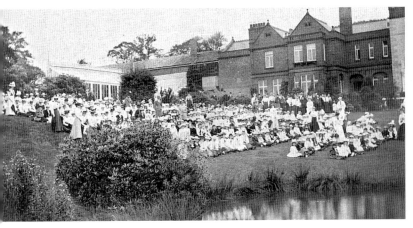

Another view of the assembly on the rectory lawns. This photograph also gives a good impression of the size of the Victorian rectory house (which was rebuilt in 1887 for Rector Hutton) set in extensive grounds and a rural location. After Hutton's retirement a smaller house was used.

Standish Walking Day, 1920s, from the same location as on p.72. The tramway (closed 1931), is still in place.

Rectory Lane, 1920s, possibly the same walking day as above. The rear of 'Spite Row' can be seen (top right), which was demolished in 1930.

Church Lane, Shevington, c. 1930: walking days were popular throughout the Wigan area.

A decorated horse drawn float at an unidentified location in Shevington, possibly the same walking day as above. Note the banner of St Anne's church, which was consecrated in 1887; the walk was held thereafter on its anniversary. The route included Lower Ground and Crooke. Harry Fisher (fourth left) and Harold Houghton (second right) have been identified.

Left: Shevington Walking Day, *c.* 1930, from the Plough & Harrow, Broad o'th'Lane.

Below: Shevington Walking Day *c.* 1930, at an unidentified location. The brass band was probably from Crooke.

Shevington Walking Day, Broad o'th'Lane, 24 July 1948.

Shevington Walking Day, *c.* 1950.

Above: Walking days were adopted by all denominations. Here, a smaller parade accompanies Crooke Methodist Sunday School, *c.* 1950.

Left: Standish's connection with the Mayflower expedition has long been celebrated in Standish. However, Myles Standish, remembered on this banner in the Market Place (probably another view from the series of about 1910), may never have seen the village. He was probably descended from the Ormskirk branch of the family, although he chose Duxbury as the name for the Pilgrim Fathers' settlement, after the Duxbury Standishes.

Eight

Local Services

Members of Standish Urban District Council at Ashfield House, 1910. Ashfield was bought by the Council in 1953, but had been used for County Council and war emergency services since the 1940s, and from 1936 by a Quaker unemployment relief society. By the 1960s it housed most of the offices and the school and child welfare clinics. When Standish became part of Wigan Metro in 1974 it continued in public use, but was sold in the 1990s for commercial use.

War Memorial Committee at the unveiling of the memorial, in front of the Globe Hotel next to the Victoria Jubilee drinking fountain, 17 April 1920. Henry Fairhurst (seated, second left), a founder member of Standish UDC, performed the ceremony. The memorial is unusual in acknowledging that hostilities continued in other theatres after the Armistice of 1918.

Coronation Celebrations Committee in front of the water tower, Green Lane, 12 May 1937. Between 1926 and 1936 over 500 new houses were built and nearly 900 old ones connected to the mains, rendering the supply inadequate; the gravity tower and new reservoirs were opened 18 July 1936, originally to mark the coronation of Edward VIII, but after his abdication a separate committee was formed to celebrate George VI's coronation. Note the 'owl and rat' relief on the lintel: this is the crest of the Standish family, and can be seen also on the parish church and the Boar's Head Inn.

Standish UDC Market Place Improvements Committee, 31 March 1930, in front of the parish church (see p. 13). Standing, left to right: Coun. E. Ashton, J.H. Richards (UDC Clerk), Coun. A. Naylor, Coun. J. Baron, Peter Moss (Contractor), Coun. G. Mather, Coun. M. Prendergast, A.A Smith (Surveyor). Seated: Coun. R. Finney, Coun. L. Cunningham, Coun. J. Baxter, Coun. B. Park, Coun. Mrs. A. Bottomley, Coun. S. Mason.

Standish Works private fire brigade, c. 1890. 'Standish Works' was the name given to the bleach works of Thomas Taylor & Co. during the 1880s (see p. 44).

Another view of the fire engine. Although Wigan borough provided a public fire service from the 1840s, small urban districts such as Standish had no public service at that time.

Sluices at Worthington Reservoir, *c.* 1950. This was one of three reservoirs built between 1855 and 1872 for Wigan Corporation Waterworks to supply the growing town. The river Douglas was culverted beneath the reservoirs and harnessed to supply the paper mill and bleach works. Now called Worthington Lakes, this a popular area for quiet recreation. In the distance is Adlington Hall.

Water tower and works from the cricket field, 1950. The concrete tower is 60' high. Note the two air-raid shelters on the left, surviving from the Second World War. The cricket ground was purchased for Standish Cricket Club in 1922 from the Standish estate.

The opening of any new facility for the community was attended by public ceremony. New vestry buildings for Standish parish church were dedicated in April 1914. They were designed by the renowned church architects Austin & Paley of Lancaster, who were described by Pevsner as 'of the highest European standard of their years.'

Sale of work (bazaar) committee at Shevington parish room, 1 February 1930. The bazaar (opened by Lord Crawford) raised funds to pay for the new parish playing field. Left to right: Mr H. Hubbard, Mr J. Roper, Mr M.B. Taylor, Revd H.S. Crabtree (vicar of St. Anne's and chairman), Mr J. Lyon (Secretary), Sir Henry Darlington (Playing Fields Association), the Earl of Crawford, Mr T.E. Hampson (Wigan RDC), Mr W.J. Griffin.

Dedication of the new war memorial at the village green, Shevington, Remembrance Sunday (9 November) 1952. The site had been given to the parish by Theobald Dixon of Shevington Hall, and the stone was donated by local quarry owners. The memorial was for parishioners killed in both World Wars.

The procession of veterans to the dedication ceremony.

Left: Sam Mason (1886-1951), chairman of Standish UDC 1937-38. Mason was the archetypal local citizen: lifelong Standish resident, educated at the village school, colliery worker (later insurance agent), councillor for 25 years (thrice chairman), magistrate and Oddfellow. Note the 'owl and rat' device on the pendant. Like other small towns, Standish became an Urban District under the Local Government Act of 1894, having had a Local Board since 1872. Major services such as education, health and highways were provided by the County Council through devolved local committees.

Below: Standish Council offices, High Street, 1989, shortly before demolition. Used as the village clinic in its last years, this had been built by the Local Board in 1893. After most departments transferred to Ashfield House in the 1950s it became known as the Public Hall, but the council chamber was retained for Council meetings. The original Local Board offices were in the Market Place.

Chorley By-Election, 1903.
THE CONSERVATIVE CANDIDATE.

Photo. by Beresford, London.

Printed and Published by S. Fowler and Sons, "Guardian" Office, Chorley.

David, Lord Lindsay, son of 26th Earl of Crawford of Haigh Hall, in his by-election leaflet for the Chorley Division of North Lancashire, 1903. Standish and Shevington were both in the Chorley constituency until after the First World War, when they were transferred to the Ince Division, and then to Westhoughton. Lindsay used Balcarres as a courtesy title. He was MP from 1895 to 1913, when he inherited the earldom and the Haigh estate. He subsequently became a government minister and a policy maker in the arts and the BBC.

Standish Branch Library, Cross Street, c. 1971. Until 1974 libraries were a county service, and Lancashire had provided a branch library in the UDC offices on High Street. In the 1930s this was open three days per week. Plans were laid for a new building, but not until 1965 was the Cross Street library built on the site of one of Standish's large old houses, White Hall.

Adventurous participants enjoy a historical cruise along the Leeds Liverpool Canal, 10 October 1995. Such events have become a popular feature of the annual Standish Festival of Arts. The Festival, which began in 1987, celebrates music, literature, crafts and the history of the district. It has become a major force in securing the cultural identity of the villages in the post-industrial era.

Nine

Getting There

Three eras of transport, Douglas Valley at Gathurst, c. 1980. The Liverpool canal was opened
as far as Wigan in 1781, largely replacing the Douglas Navigation; the river is below the canal to
the left. The train is crossing the viaduct of the Wigan-Southport line which opened in 1855.
Towering above all is the road viaduct spanning the whole valley, built between 1959 and 1962
to carry the second section of the M6 motorway opened on 29 July 1963.

Left: Cast iron mile post at Boar's Head, Standish, 1998. Between the late seventeenth and mid-nineteenth centuries most main roads in Britain were maintained by Turnpike Trusts, set up by private Acts of Parliaments. Trusts charged tolls and erected gates and bars to collect them. In 1727 the Wigan-Preston (South of Yarrow) Trust was established to maintain the present A49 and A5106 roads. This post is one of a series erected in 1837 in Standish parish along these roads, possibly to celebrate Queen Victoria's accession.

Below: Leeds Liverpool Canal at Dean Locks, Gathurst, by Revd William Wickham, 1915. Between the coal barges is the Wigan Coal & Iron Co.'s steam tug *Scotland*, one of four towing vessels acquired in 1914 and named after the home countries. This view gives a good impression of how busy the canal remained with coal traffic well into this century, despite competition from the railways.

Horse-drawn coal boats at Gathurst in the early 1900s, by William Wickham.

Canal near Gathurst, 1960s, showing how things had changed since Wickham's time. Elderly unpowered craft such as *Bruno* were still in use for coal but were now towed by motor boat. The M6 viaduct had recently been built. Note also the summer houses on the canal bank (right) coverted from old buses and wagons shacks, which have only recently disappeared.

Railway viaducts across the Douglas Valley near Boar's Head, early 1900s. A view north-west of the Whelley loop line passing beneath the line between Boar's Head and Chorley which forms the background of this photograph. The latter was in 1869 by Lancashire Union Railway, the Whelley opening in 1882.

View north-east from the other side of the Whelley loop viaduct showing contrasting construction methods. It was built by London & North Western Railway Co. in 1882 to connect with the main line at Standish, forming a Wigan by-pass route. The Douglas here marks the Wigan-Standish parish boundary.

The approach to Standish railway station from Rectory Lane, c. 1910. The station was served by local trains on the west coast main line, but was a mile from the village. Opened in 1838 by Lancashire Union Railway, it was originally called Standish Lane station.

Standish station, c. 1910, looking north. In 1895 the tracks were doubled from two to four, at the height of the west coast line's usage. Those seen here served north bound trains, an additional platform and two more tracks serving southbound traffic beyond the building to the right. Standish station was closed on 23 May 1949, and in 1972 the line reduced again to two tracks.

Above: Boar's Head junction in the mid-1950s, and a southbound main line train hauled by a Princess class locomotive. The tracks curving away to the right are those of the line to Blackburn via Chorley, opened in 1869. Boar's Head station, with platforms serving both lines, was closed on 31 January 1949.

Left: Standish junction signal box, at the north end of the island platform (see p. 95). Dating from the doubling of the main line in 1895, it replaced an earlier box south of the station. Along with neighbouring boxes and semaphore signals it was rendered obsolete during the electrification of the line in 1972-73.

The coming of trams made travelling into Wigan easier for ordinary Standish folk. Boar's Head was first served on 16 May 1902 when Wigan Corporation's narrow gauge line was extended from Elmfield Road. In 1905 it was re-built to standard gauge and extended to High Street. This view shows car 76, one of thirty new vehicles ordered for the new system, at the Boar's Head stop.

Boar's Head petrol filling station and garage. Developed in the 1920s to attract the rapidly increasing traffic at the busy junction of Wigan Road and Chorley Road, this was originally owned independently by J.F. Worswick; by 1941 it had been bought by City Petroleum Co. The price of petrol (ls 4d per gallon), suggests a date of about 1930.

Langtree Garage, Preston Road, in the 1930s, owned then by William Whitehill. Situated next to Saddle Hill farm, opposite the old Quaker burial ground, this was one of several garages that sprang up as motor traffic increased along the A49. Another was Delph garage by Avondale Road (Andrews brothers), which had opened in about 1929, shortly before Langtree.

Another view of Langtree Garage from across the recently macadamized A49.

Proprietors and employees of Shevington hauliers Ball & Yates, with their vehicles at Miles Lane, early 1930s. In the 1920s William Ball and Daniel Yates, presumably the firm's partners, were listed in directories as farmers. The Thornycroft lorry on the left bears a Wigan registration mark.

Broad o'th'Lane, Shevington, 1930s. Village centres such as this were scarcely troubled with motor traffic, and the presence of a private car in the street was still unusual. EK 4467 (a Wigan registration) was first issued in 1926.

Left: Cast iron mile post on Preston Road, Standish, following restoration, 1998. One of seven surviving posts erected in 1837 (see p. 92), these were cast at Haigh Foundry (several bear the legend 'Haigh Foundry'), and all bear the name of the township in which they were situated.

Below: Public and private transport in Church Lane, Shevington, mid-1950s. The Wigan registered Ford Popular car and the single deck Ribble bus were both new in 1952. The latter (fleet no. 392), is a Leyland Royal Tiger bound for Wigan on the 333 service. In the background is one of Ribble's double deckers emerging from Broad o' th' Lane.

Ten

Are You Being Served?

Boar's Head Inn, Standish, early 1900s, before the addition of the modern gables. Dating from the 15th century the Boar's Head is situated at a busy junction on the road from Wigan to Preston, which was turnpiked in 1726. It features in Robert Neill's historical novel *Moon in Scorpio*. Like most of the pubs in the village at this period it was owned by the Standish brewer J.B. Almond.

Old Seven Stars Inn, Langtree. Also on the Wigan-Preston road, this was an inn at least in the eighteenth century: a maid called Temperance was sent by the churchwardens to fetch wine. The licence was transferred to another Old Seven Stars (opposite James Square) in the late 1800s. Meanwhile a New Seven Stars (previously The Yew Tree), was opened opposite the building shown here!

Victoria Bowling Green Inn, Miles Lane, Shevington, c. 1914. The man in the porch may have been the last licensee, William Gore. By that time it was a beer house, for which it was cheaper and easier to get a licence. The building subsequently became the Conservative Club.

Globe Inn, at the junction of Church Street and High Street, Standish, *c.* 1920. Previously a beer house, by 1914 it had a full licence. Whittle Springs was a Chorley brewery, taken over by Matthew Brown (Nuttall's) in 1928.

Dog & Partridge Inn (beer house), School Lane, Standish, early 1900s. The pub still flourishes though the old houses either side have been demolished. Nearly all of Oldfield's houses were in Wigan; it was taken over by Walker's in 1926.

An off-licence at 68-69, Standish Lower Ground, early 1900s. This was Oldfield's only other house in Standish. It was ideally situated to quench the thirsts of the miners of Douglas Bank, many of whom lived in the terraced cottages along Lower Road built in the late 1800s by Wigan Coal & Iron Co.

Eagle & Child Inn, Market Place, Standish, early 1900s. Another of Almond's houses, this one lost its licence, said to date from at least 1703, in 1916 when the authorities considered it too small and surplus to the village's needs. Matthias Speakman was the last licensee. In the early eighteenth century the property included a house and adjoining shop, garden, orchard and over twelve customary acres of land.

Worthington's butchers shop, c. 1980. Now a private house this is, for most readers, the most familiar guise of the former Eagle & Child.

Above: Williams Deacon's Bank, at the corner of High Street and Market Street, Standish, 1930s. Opened in 1894 in a former furniture shop, the branch was open three days a week and by 1914 had over 100 accounts. The name was changed to Williams & Glyn's in 1970 and to Royal Bank of Scotland in 1985, though the latter had bought the Deacon's share capital in 1929. The shop adjoining was Wildings, newsagents.

Left: Post Office, Gathurst Lane, *c.* 1900. Shevington had other sub-post offices at Crooke, Shevington Moor and Broad o'th' Lane. The Gathurst sub-post mistress at this time was a Mrs Sutherland. There was a daily collection of post (including Sundays) and one daily delivery. There was also a telegraph service (see p. 19).

Above: Samuel Hale's grocer's and
butcher's shop, Market Place, Standish,
c. 1910. Originally the residence of Miss
Smalley (see p. 53), it was converted to
shop premises in the early 1900s by J.M.
Ainscough (see p. 13) and then acquired
by Hale, who kept the shop until his death
in 1937. It was continued by his daughters
until 1959, and subsequently demolished.

Right: George Marsh, a paper boy in
Shevington in the 1920s.

Lil's Cafe, Preston Road, Standish, 1963. Perhaps not the Standish chapter of Hell's Angels but obviously a popular rendezvous for bikers in the 1960s. Situated towards the Coppull end of Preston Road adjoining the New Seven Stars, the cafe was ideal for riders who built up a lick of speed coming down from Standish. It is now an Asian restaurant.

Eleven

At Play

G A M E.

WHEREAS the GAME within the Manors, Lordſhips, and Townſhips of *Standiſh cum Langtree, Shevington,* and *Wrightington,* has for a long Time paſt been very much deſtroyed by Perſons ſporting thereon without Leave, and by Poachers:

Notice is hereby given,

THAT the Lords of the ſaid Manor and Owners of Eſtates in the above Places, have entered into an ASSOCIATION to proſecute all Poachers; and in as much as the GAME the laſt Year has bred very ill, and has been almoſt deſtroyed by the wet Seaſon, the Gamekeepers have Orders to kill no more GAME, and all qualified Perſons are requeſted to deſiſt ſporting thereon this Seaſon, and at all Times in future without firſt obtaining a written Licence from the Lords.

A notice prohibiting the taking of game within Standish, Shevington and Wrightington, *c.* 1780; a popular recreation amongst landowners and tenants, and a source of profit and food for poachers. Game had apparently been depleted by illegal sport and by 'the wet season'.

Standish Grammar School football club, 1898/9, photographed in front of the old school building on Green Lane.

Standish Church Lads' Brigade footballers, 1905, photographed at the Grammar School.

Standish Juniors football club, *c.* 1920.

Standish Cricket team and officers, 1928. The Cricket Club celebrated its centenary in 1977 and has enjoyed great recent success. In 1901 it hired a professional player-cum-groundsman at 25s. per week, and recruited subsequently from the Midlands and London. In 1914 Standish won the Wigan League title. Rector Hutton was President from 1894 to 1938.

Shevington Church (St Anne's) football club, 1921-22. Standing, left to right; G. Stopforth, W. Osborne, Jimmy Tyrer, H. Chadwick, T. Fisher, J Sharpe, J. Speakman, Tommy Tyrer. Seated: W. Houghton, R. Fairclough, C. Dodd, T. Bennett, W. Parkinson, N. Brown, T. Parkinson, W. Osborne.

Shevington Church football club, 1929/30. Back row, left to right: John Brown, Tommy Tyrer, Percy Gaskell, Jimmy Culshaw. Middle row: -?-, W. Lee, Bob Ashcroft, Jack Spencer, Albert Shovelton. Front row: Joe Roberts, J. Worthington, Revd Crabtree (vicar), R. Ellwood (captain), H. Stewart, H. Robinson, Fred Rigby.

Shevington Tennis Club, 1930s. Standing, left to right: H. Lomax, Mr. Griffin, -?-, -?-, Fred Rigby, Adam Rigby. Seated: Mabel Hesketh, Mr Taylor, -?-, Revd Crabtree (vicar), Molly Lomax, James Lyon, Annie Rigby.

Bowlers from 'The Bone Hole', British Glues Ltd's factory by the canal in Shevington, at a fixture held at Shevington Conservative Club, July 1952.

Parishioners of St Anne's, Shevington, enjoying a day out (location unknown) in about 1910.

Shevington May Queen pageant, c. 1930.

Garden party at 'Greenhill', Gathurst Lane (now Princes Park), Shevington in about 1938:
Wigan's mayor for 1937-38, Ernest Ball (centre) was evidently guest of honour. Greenhill was
the home of Robert Alstead (1873-1946; third right), founder of Alsteads, the Wigan clothiers.
He was also a leading Liberal councillor 1913-29, mayor 1926, MP for Altrincham 1923/4 and
candidate in Wigan and Preston. He is buried at St Anne's.

Workers from the Roburite explosives factory at Gathurst enjoying a charabanc outing, c. 1930.

Members of Standish scout troop at camp, 25 June 1914.

Opening of a new headquarters building for the 1st Shevington Scout Group, Whitehall Avenue, 25th April 1983. Group Leader Fred Green (centre), receives a plate to mark his dedication to the cause.

Twelve

The People

An Edwardian family group: a gathering of the numerous Ball family at Tan Pit farm,
Shevington, c. 1910. Edward Ball (seated, centre), was an overseer and guardian of the poor,
chairman of both Shevington Parish and Wigan Rural District Councils and a local magistrate.
He died in 1914.

Left: Emily Little of 1, Collingwood Street, Standish in the early 1900s.

Below: The Hooten children of Broad o'th' Lane, *c.* 1906. Left to right: Jack, Helena, Teresa, Alice.

Opposite: The Finch family at Robin Hill farm, Standish, *c.* 1914 (see p. 41).

Tom Little of Shevington, 1918.

Mr and Mrs Johnson and children Flo and Jim, at their home 'The Poplars', Shevington, 6 February 1916.

Above: Mr and Mrs Griffin and son, Shevington, 1915.

Left: Jack and Hannah Scholfield (nee Jerstice) of Standish: a wedding portrait of about 1920.

Above: John Jerstice (seated, centre). Born in Chorley he came to Standish to work as a contractor and shaft-sinker at Langtree Colliery, and between 1899 and 1906 held the licence at the Hind's Head pub, Wrightington. He lived latterly at 245, Bradley Lane.

Right: Four generations of a Shevington family, *c.* 1927: Eric Little and his mother Alice, grandmother Hooten and great grandmother Hodkinson.

Left: Julie Simm, a red cross nurse at The Beeches, School Lane, Standish, which was used as a military hospital in the First World War.

Below: Theobald Dixon with his grand-niece Caroline Todd in the garden at Shevington New Hall, c. 1936 (see p35). Dixon came to Lancashire in 1875 and made a career with Thomas Taylor's cotton spinning business at Victoria Mills, Wigan. He moved to Shevington Hall in the early 1900s, and is recalled today as a beneficent gentleman by the daughter of his last housekeeper and gardener, in the latter days of the small country house. He died in 1954, aged 97.

Above: A Standish family group at Bradley Lane Cottages, 1930s.

Right: Revd H.S. Crabtree (vicar of Shevington 1928-1964) with Mrs Tyrer, about 1945, possibly at the VE Day celebrations. Harold Crabtree was Shevington's third and longest serving incumbent, a sporting bachelor (see pp. 112-13) who spent his summer holidays as an umpire at Wimbledon.

To Annie & Dick
with best wishes &
kind remembrance
Eva Turner London

Daguerre

The ancient graveyard at Standish parish church has received some notable burials, none more so than that of Eva Turner in 1990, whose ashes were brought from London to be put with her parents' grave. Born in 1892, Turner became one of Britain's finest operatic sopranos, her powerful voice bringing her a wide range of parts. This portrait shows her as Aida at Chicago in 1930.

Thomas Cruddas Porteus, vicar of Coppull (one of the old chapelries of Standish parish) between 1912 and 1934. Porteus was a notable local historian and antiquary. His *History of the Parish of Standish* (1927) and his accurate edition of the Standish family deeds are wonderful mines of information about the district.

Mr J. Snape, a foreman in the Roburite factory at Gathurst photographed about 1928 with a splendid gramophone, presumably his retirement gift.

Acknowledgements

The author wishes to thank the following members of the staff of Wigan Heritage Service for research on various sections of the book: Bob Blakeman (At Home, At Prayer); Dawn Wadsworth (At School, Are You Being Served ?); Mike Haddon (At Work, Getting There).

Thanks also to Len Hudson for the photography.

Thanks to all donors, depositors and lenders of photographs and to suppliers of information, without whom this book would not have been possible. Specifically among these thanks to: J. Keith, Harry Entwistle, Adrian Morris, the Finch family, Canon Paul Warren (Rector of Standish), Miss F. Pilkington, I. Lewis, the Little family, Mrs M. Martin, Mrs E. Dickinson, Bernard Catterall.

The photograph on p.106 of Williams Deacon's Bank is reproduced by kind permission of The Royal Bank of Scotland plc.